MW01169375

Mini Book Model

How to Write Your Big Ideas in Small Books

Chris Stanley

Stanley Crew LLC

Contents

BONUS

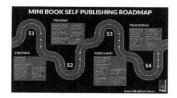

Ready to publish your mini book with confidence? The Mini Book Success Checklist is your step-by-step guide to making it happen. (inclues bonus resources for every step!)

Here's what you'll find inside:

- Prepping Guide: Craft a compelling title, subtitle, and outline that capture your readers' attention.

- Penning Checklist: Break down your book into manageable chapters and sections, ensuring smooth and efficient writing.

- Publishing Blueprint: Get your book formatted, uploaded, and ready for sale with ease.

- Promotion Plan: Learn the key strategies to launch your

book, attract readers, and gain reviews.

- Downloadable Printer Friendly PDF (with checkable boxes)

- Notion checklist (for those who love staying organized in Notion software)

Head to MiniBookModel.com

Introduction

You aren't just writing a book.
You're building a machine that prints money and credibility.
If you're not just an author, but a Revenue Writer, this is how you win.

The old way? Dead.

Readers don't want 80,000 words, they want **breakthroughs** in one hour.
They want speed, clarity, and transformation they can act on now.

Your Mini Book becomes the **engine** that drives your authority, your audience, and your income.

You don't need a publishing deal.
You don't need 10,000 followers.
You don't need six months of content strategy.

This isn't a book, it's leverage.
It's a business blueprint disguised as a book.

Write faster. Publish smarter. Lap the old way until it's a dot in your rearview mirror.

The Big Book Lie

We've all been sold a dream:
That writing a "real" book means 40,000 words, expensive editors, fancy launch strategies, and months (or years) of pain.

It's the same playbook whether you go traditional or "self-publish."

Self-publishing was supposed to be freedom. But for most, it's just **doing traditional publishing alone, with none of the help, and all the pain**.

You're told to:

- Spend $3,000+ on editing.

- Hire cover designers and typesetters.

- Appear on 100 podcasts.

- Maybe land a morning TV slot if you're lucky.

That's not practical.
That's delusional.

Real people can't do that.
Busy parents can't do that.
Aspiring revenue writers shouldn't even try.

And here's the kicker:

Why?
Because traditional nonfiction is too long.

Big books don't get read.
Big books don't get finished.
Big books don't build momentum fast enough in the AI age.

That's the **Big Book Lie...** and it's time to bury it.

Practical Publishing Is the Future

You don't need a legacy nonfiction book.
You need a **Mini Book.**

Short, sharp, and shippable.

Mini Books are built for busy readers *and* busy writers.

They are:

- Readable in one sitting

- Authored in one week

- Profitable from day one

No fluff. No filler. No waiting around.

This is **Practical Publishing**:
A new way to turn expertise into income and impact fast.

The 7-Stages of Building Your Mini Book Revenue Machine

Here's how it works:
You're not just writing a book, (well you could just write a book, but for those that want to do and earn more with a business) you're building a revenue machine in disguise.

Each stage of the system builds speed, traction, and momentum. Each piece connects to the next.

1. **Niche (Chassis)** — Decide what you're building and who it's for. *(This book.)*

2. **Mini Book (Engine)** — Create the asset that powers your business. (Mini Book Writing[1])

3. **Marketing (Transmission)** — Deliver your message with force to spin those wheels. (Mini Book Publishing[2] & Mini

---

1. https://www.amazon.com/gp/product/B0DYF38R8C

Book Marketing)[3])

4. **Products (Tires)** — Build offers that give you traction.

5. **Brand (Body)** — Shape the body that turns heads and is remembered.

6. **Metrics (Dashboard)** — Track your speed and direction.

7. **Community (Fuel)** — Fuel your machine with superfans.

But here's the part most people miss.

Without the chassis, you have nowhere to bolt the machine.

Your niche and strategy is the foundation. It decides your audience, your message, your product. It's the steel frame that holds everything together. Most people skip this step, because they're scared to choose. They want to keep their options open.

They want to appeal to everyone... and end up invisible to everyone.

This book is Stage 1 — **Building Your Chassis**.

Own this strategy.
We'll help you pick your lane.

Define your audience.

Decide the specific problem you solve.

Your Mini Book forces clarity.

Forces positioning.

Forces power.

Get this right, and the rest of the machine builds itself. Miss it, and nothing else you do will matter. This is where the real race begins.

Start your engines.

Authors Note

My only regret after getting 100+ reviews on this book?
Not seeing the whole picture from day one.

I knew the Mini Book Model worked. I used it to launch products, build credibility, and generate real revenue. Not millions or jet planes, but $750,000/year from a "boring" niche writing books about insurance adjusting. (*Yawn*, right?) Income that brought my family freedom.

I hadn't taken the time to name the system.
I hadn't connected the dots.

Now I have.

What you're reading is **Stage 1 of the Mini Book Revenue Machine**.
The new introduction in this book gave you the full lens.

I'm not hiding this behind a paywall, webinar funnel, or overpriced coaching program. I'm giving it to you because it works. And because the world doesn't need more authors.

It needs more Revenue Writers.

Hit the gas. Turn the page.

Chris Stanley (the Mini Book Guy)
19x Amazon #1 Best Seller

Chapter 1

What is a Mini Book (and Why It's Your First Business Move)

A new format of writing has arrived.

It arrived out of necessity for readers. The way people consume content is changing, and the creator does not get to decide how people consume content. Authors can only decide if they want to reach those who demand new formats. While legacy non-fiction books remain popular, a shift is happening in our culture, as people demand new and shorter forms of content. The success of TikTok and Twitter reveals that people want content at a faster pace. The writing formats that most writers are familiar with don't satisfy this fast paced craving of readers.

Let's look at the different digital writing formats and how they serve different purposes.

Different Digital Writing Formats

You can tell a reader the same thing in lots of different ways.

You can write a Tweet, blog post, thread, record a video or a podcast. You can host a Zoom meeting to inform a reader of the point you want to make. We can communicate to a reader through so many options and formats, but each serve a unique purpose and has different benefits.

Below are the major forms of digital writing, a quick summation, the average word counts, shelf life, and how long it typically takes to create.

Social Post
Quick to write, instant distribution, worldwide audience, short shelf life.

Shelf Life: Short

Time to Write: 1-120 minutes

Word Count: 1-500 words

Blog Post

More in depth than a social post and more prep time. No audience except the one you have or search engine visibility you generate.

Shelf Life: Medium

Time to Write: 1 minute to day(s)

Word Count: 250-2500 words

Newsletter

Comparable to a blog post in terms of the amount of content, the layout, and the time taken to prepare it. An email newsletter is great because it already has a built-in audience, and it's a direct connection to the reader.

Shelf Life: Short (full inbox)

Time to Write: 1 hour to 1 day

Word Count: 250 – 2500 words

Non-Fiction Book

Deeply researched, extreme prep time, audience is at digital and physical bookstores or your website. You can promote on social, blog, and your email list.

Shelf Life: Years to Decades

Time to Write: Months to Years

Word Count: 30,000 – 80,000 words

Ebook

Ebooks have been the catch all for digital versions of books, blog posts, and a range of other lengths of material. Any writing that is electronic or "E" has had ebook slapped onto it. Because of this, most readers devalue "ebooks" because it is hard to define the format and can be a gamble for the reader.

Shelf Life: Short to Years

Time to Write: Hours to Years

Word Count: 250-80,000 words

That is the typical hierarchy of digitally written content.

The last format, ebooks, is a moving target. But did you notice a gigantic leap in the word count? We went from 2500 words for a newsletter and blog post to 30,000 words for a non-fiction book. As an author, this gap always frustrated me.

I had more to say than a blog post, but 30,000 words is a lot to ask someone to read or for an author to write on a subject.

I knew historically there had been shorter non-fiction books that have greatly benefited society.

Thomas Paine's Common Sense was only 20,000 words and helped spark the American Revolution. The wisest man that lived, Solomon, wrote his masterpiece, Proverbs, in 15,000 words. Napoleon Hill wrote a booklet titled Magic Ladder of Success in 1921. In that smaller work, he revealed for the first time his framework that eventually led to his book masterpiece, Think and Grow Rich. Yet, we as authors hold ourselves to a word count of 30,000 for non-fiction books.

Why is that?

Because traditionally published books needed to look fat on a shelf to make readers feel it was worth purchasing. With readers consuming books digitally and craving quick media, it's time to rethink our word counts and to give ourselves permission to write shorter books and give readers the opportunity to read them.

It's time for the era of the mini book.

How is a Mini Book Different?

A mini book is highly consumable fast paced book that makes good on the promise to the reader with no fluff.

The most obvious difference between a legacy non-fiction book and mini book is word count.

Mini books unshackle the author and allow them to write a published book with 5000 words or more. The authors leading the charge on mini books, Category Pirates, typically write between 5000 and 10,000 word count for their works. Mini book is the format that is filling the gap between newsletters/blog posts and legacy non-fiction books.

A mini book is anything between 5,000 and 15,000 words.

There are other differences with mini books as well.

Because of the restriction, or liberation in word count, the topic being written about must fit the container you are trying to put your ideas into.

Mini books have 1 interesting topic, question, or idea that dominates the pages. While a legacy non-fiction book may tell you "How to Be an Accountant" and everything that it entails. A mini book would pick up and analyze just one aspect of being an accountant. The topic idea might be, "How to Organize Your Desk as an Accountant", or "Quit Using QuickBooks: Why It's Ruining Your Accounting Business".

Mini books are a singular idea versus a slew of ideas.

You might think to yourself, "I've read lots of non-fiction books that only had one idea stretched across the pages."

Exactly, but those books should have been mini books or blog posts. The author expanded the word count to fulfill the contract with the publisher. Most readers don't make it all the way through those books. 60% or more of books that are started don't get finished.

I'd argue that it isn't because the author's topic, ideas, or words weren't interesting, but because it just took too long for the reader to finish and receive the promised payoff.

We've all read a book where we got the gist of the entire book 1/4 of the way through, in 10,000 words or less and quit reading, that is why I believe mini books are here to stay.

A Mini Book is Your POV

A mini book is perfect for representing an author's point of view.

Your point of view (POV) is what will carry the mini book and the reader to completion. The best mini books have one clear point of view,

- Don't use QuickBooks

- Your Personal Brand Isn't Helping Anyone

- Category Design is the Key to Growing Your Business

- Etc.

While most legacy non-fiction books try to cover everything there is to cover on a topic just to fill the page count, a mini book sticks to the POV at which they wrote it from and doesn't chase bunny trails.

Mini books are quick and concise.

Authors fill Mini books with hooks, punches, and finishing lines that leave the reader desperate for more. It's a more entertaining form of non-fiction book writing, which also makes it more challenging for the author than a matter-of-fact blog post. The brevity and singular focus forces the author to abandon long prose and drawn out stories.

Now that you know what a mini book is, let's look at why you need to write one.

Chapter 2

Who Writes and Who Reads Mini Books

There have been shorter books written in the legacy non-fiction space dating back thousands of years.

With the rise of the ebook, modern authors have joined in on writing shorter books, but thanks to the dilution and non-standard format of length, a reader doesn't know what to expect when they hear the word ebook. With the rise of mini books, this gives authors and readers a way to categorize and communicate shorter non-fiction books.

Some authors have already begun making huge strides to advance mini books to the front.

None more so than Category Pirates.

The writing band of Nicolas Cole, Christopher Lochhead and Eddie Yoon have been producing mini books every month for the past two years. They've burst onto the scene and taken the business book industry by surprise with their success at writing what used to be thought of as "laughably" short books.

There are no shortage of short non-fiction ebooks on the internet.

Many of these are authors and thought leaders that built multi six figure or seven-figure businesses on the backs of their short non-fiction works. These authors of short books just didn't have a good name for their short format.

I co-authored a book with a friend of mine, John Bachmann, about how to get a job as an adjuster at an insurance company (legacy non-fiction catch all topic). When we wrote the book, it became apparent that the section on prepping a resume was ballooning to an enormous size. We spun it off as a separate, laser focused short book. Although we didn't know to call it a mini book, that is exactly what it was.

That shorter book on the super niche topic of adjuster resumes sold 2x more than the comprehensive book on how to get a job at an insurance company.

The People Who Would Benefit Most From Writing a Mini Book

Certain authors will benefit more from writing a mini book more than others.

- **First-Time Authors:** A mini book is a great way to break the ice. You can learn the writing and publishing process while coming out the other side with something you can be proud of. You can do it in a fraction of the time it'll take to write a legacy non-fiction book.

- **Business Owners:** If you own a business, share your point of view with the world. A mini book is a great way to do that. What better way to help your clients or earn new customers than to author a mini book on what it is you can help them with.

- **Thought Leaders/Personalities:** With the rise of internet stardom, lots of people are turning to social media to establish credibility in their career or as coaches, mentors, consultants, etc. A mini book is a perfect way to show your leading thoughts. Just make sure your ideas sound different from others if you want to win people over.

- **Marketers:** There is no better way to start your sales funnel than with a mini book. Readers can price check your book on Amazon and see that you are indeed giving them a special offer and you can begin a relationship with them as you guide them through your sales funnel by giving them tremendous value through your mini book.

If you've ever thought "I should write a non-fiction book," you absolutely should.

I'm here to give you permission to start small, heck, even start mini and write a mini book. Even if you want to author a memoir of your life, you could start by just telling one story, one year, or one era of your life with a mini book.

Remove the burden of word count and get writing.

The People You'll Be Able to Reach

Who is going to read a mini book?

People who care about the problem you solve or the thoughts you propose in your book. People don't buy books based on the size of the book. I'd argue that more readers are averse to big books than drawn to them.

In every other aspect of life, we as consumers want the quickest solution possible.

People buy a non-fiction book as a remedy, a medicine for a problem they are experiencing in their lives. They don't care how long it is. They just care that it actually solves their problem and provides the information promised.

The people that will read your mini books are,

- **Your Fans:** Your email list and social media following will gobble up your mini book if you've been providing value to them.

- **Your Industry:** Your industry needs people to write books about their industry. While it may not go on the big best-seller lists, a book about sprinklers makes you a favorite among the landscaping community.

- **Online Bookstores:** One of the greatest places to expand your audience and find new readers is through Amazon, Barnes and Noble, Kobo, Apple, Google, and the other online bookstores. With 300 million self-published books sold a year, you can find readers.

If you are doubting whether someone will read a mini book, I want you to think about the last time you bought an "ebook" on Amazon or a website and did you actually think about how many pages or words were in it? Normally you can't tell and don't care, because you just want your problem solved.

As long as the author solves the problem, a reader is fine with whatever length the book is.

Chapter 3

Why You Should Write a Mini Book

As you consider this mini book format, you may wonder why you would write one.

I could write an entire mini book just on that topic alone! But I'll do my best to give you some compelling reasons here. I believe strongly that writing a book is life-changing as an author.

Chandler Bolt of Self Publishing School says "Books change the lives of the readers and the authors" and it's so true.

Present Your POV to the World

The main reason I want you to write a mini book is so you get it done.

I believe you have something to share with the world and with 97% of books abandoned by the authors, I'm trying to bring that completion percentage up. Your point of view, experiences, and lessons learned can help other people.

We just need to get the thoughts out of your head and onto the page for a reader to love.

Your point of view is radically different from other authors in your space.

Readers are looking for new ways of doing things, different options and ways to tackle problems they face. The only options they find are the ones who are brave enough to hit publish. You can be one of them.

You should write a mini book to give your POV to the world.

How Mini Books Can Help Grow Your Business

If you are a business owner, solopreneur, or marketer, write a book.

If you don't want to wait months or years to finish a legacy non-fiction book, mini books are a great way to inject excitement, buzz, and income into your business. When a company has written the book (and not just an ebook) on the topic, it lends them tremendous amounts of credibility.

Some of the biggest ways it can grow your business are,

- Generating new leads for your company

- Generating income from the sales of the book

- Opening doors to conferences, speaking engagements, or conversations with industry leaders you couldn't get before.

If you are trying to grow your influence in your market, a niche mini book is a fast way to do it.

The Different Reasons to Write a Mini Book

You may choose to write a mini book for many reasons.

Besides growing your business and becoming an authority on a topic, there are other reasons that come to mind.

1. Elevator Pitch of Your Company

A mini book forces you to refine your thoughts into words. It's much easier to remember something once you've written it down. Many business owners have trouble describing what they do or how they do it. Once you've written a mini book on the topic, it is easier to give a short, concise explanation.

2. Testing the Waters for a Bigger Book

If you want to write a legacy non-fiction book, you can use mini books to test the market on your idea.

You can break up your "big" book into multiple mini books. Writing and publishing smaller mini books primes the pump, gets you used to the process, and builds an audience that will be excited for your legacy non-fiction book.

3. Use Amazon and Digital Bookstore Algorithms to Rank

When you search on Google for different things, Google shows you products and websites that are related to your search.

Your book can show up in that products category and also in the search listings on the 1st page of the results. Because Amazon is such a trusted/visited site you being listed on there provides enormous SEO (search engine optimization) or visibility for your book that you would struggle to achieve on your own.

This has happened to me with my books for independent insurance adjusters.

4. As a Time Capsule

Your kids and others will want to know what you learned and experienced when you are no longer on this Earth.

Have you ever wished you could sit down and talk with your grandpa now that you are grown? I know I have. I wrote my last mini book, The Misleading Money Mantra, because I wanted my kids to know where my head was at during this period of my life.

Mini books make this possible by removing the huge barrier to completion that legacy non-fiction books put in our way.

Checkpoint

Hey, I hope you are enjoying the book and seeing how Mini Books can quickly transform you and your business.

If this book is helping you see a new path forward, I'd be honored if you left a short review on the bookstore where you purchased it.

You can also head to https://minibookmodel.com/ and click "Leave a Review" for easy access to the review page.

Now let's dive into how to actually write a mini book!

Chapter 4

How You Write a Mini Book

Since you are still reading I think it is safe for me to assume that you want to take on the task of writing a mini book.

I'll do my best to make this as simple as possible. There is little magic to writing a book. The secret sauce is in your own head with your experiences, memories, and contrarian opinions. I'll be providing you frameworks not to imprison you, but to take away the guessing game at how to get started.

If you prefer, you can do things your own way and not follow my instructions.

If considering writing mini books, you are already a rebel and a pirate, so I wouldn't expect you to blindly follow along step for step, but I can give you a map.

How to Choose a Mini Book Topic

The most important decision you make with your mini book is deciding on your topic.

Your topic and POV together are the book. Everything else is coloring in between the lines of the outline. Whether your book is interesting or not is decided before you write a single word.

Your topic is often easy to determine. It's related to your niche or market you are trying to reach.

Examples of niche are,

- Insurance adjusting

- Marketing

- Writing

- Landscaping

If you know your niche now you need to decide on the topic you want to write about.

- Insurance Adjuster Resumes

- Marketing Emails

- Writing Mini Books

- Selling Sprinkler Systems

Once you've done these two step you are close to knowing what your book will be about.

The last step is deciding your point of view, your POV. A good mini book POV is different and clear from the beginning. A boring mini book says the same thing every other book says from the same POV.

You can write about a topic hundreds of people have written before if, and only if you have a unique POV.

Examples of unique POV's are,

- Traditional marketing is a waste of time. Category design is the way to dominate up to 76% of your market.

- Using a graphical resume as an insurance adjuster is a mistake. You must use a traditional plain resume if you want to get hired.

- Writing a legacy non-fiction book is hard and takes months or years to complete. You should write a mini book first.

- You are doing a disservice by mowing your clients' grass and not offering them sprinklers.

While your point of view doesn't have to be contrarian or opposite of everyone, it helps. Whether you go with a non-obvious POV that no one has ever heard of or whether you are closer to other lines of thinking, you must be abundantly clear to yourself and your reader what your POV is.

Your POV guides the entire book and you cannot deviate from your POV in your mini book, or you risk bunny trails that confuse your reader.

Once you have your niche, topic, and POV, you should have ideas popping in your head of what you want to write about and ideas for a title.

Choosing a Title

The title of your mini book is extremely important.

It has two roles.

1. Clearly communicate what the book is about.

2. Make a promise to the reader.

Your title and subtitle together should tell the reader what your book is about and promise them what they'll get out of reading the book.

I like to choose a title and subtitle before I do any outlining. It informs me of the promise I'm making the reader. When writing I can reference back and see if I am writing content that is fulfilling that promise or not.

If your title is clever and doesn't clearly explain what your book is about, make sure your subtitle states it plainly.

For example, Category Pirates legacy non-fiction book (a collection of mini books, mind you), Snow Leopard, doesn't tell us what the book is about. It isn't until you include the subtitle, Snow Leopard: How Legendary Writers Create a Category of One, that you understand what you are about to read.

Once you have your title and subtitle, it's time to outline your mini book.

3 Easy Outlines for Mini Books

Outlining your mini book can make or break the content inside.

Without a good outline, your writing will suffer. It provides the structure and support for your writing. The outline is also there to help the reader know what they are reading and understand how it all works together.

Often we avoid simple outlines because it doesn't feel "smart", but clear outlines are the easiest and simplest way to start and easier for the reader to follow along.

Here are 3 mini outlines that I've used that will speed up your writing process.

1. **W's**

2. **10 Problems**

3. **Sequential**

Let's look at each of these and how to use them.

W's Outline Model

The good old W's outline model makes sure you cover all the important questions on a topic.

It answers the questions of,

- Who

- What

- When

- Where

- Why

- How

This mini book you are reading uses the W's outline method.

Each chapter is answering one of these questions. You can get creative on what the question is or how it's framed. For example, instead of writing "Who are Mini Books For" I used "Who Writes and Reads Mini Books?" For certain books, the W's work to prime the topic and then the "H", or "How, is what most of the book's true focus is on.

For mini books, it is a balance, but you get to decide how your book flows.

Sequential Outline Model

There are mini book subjects that fit into a sequential outline model like a glove.

When I wrote my most popular adjusting book, Independent Adjuster's Playbook, the first edition was a mini book. (I just didn't know to call it that) It was a roadmap of every step a person new to the industry needed to take to get started. Writing out the steps someone needed to take was the bulk of my outline. I started the book with anything they needed to know before they got to the steps by step.

Especially if your book is heavy on the "How" a sequential outline can work great.

10 Problems Outline Model

When writing for an established niche and topic, there is no better outline than the 10 problems.

Identify the 10 biggest things that people complain about, face, or hold them back and make each of those a chapter. This ensures you are writing a mini book that is focused and highly valuable to a niche that is looking for solutions. Being a solution driven book is a great way to make your mini book appeal to readers.

Don't worry if your chapter titles seem boring.

You can rewrite those chapter titles once you finish the content if you think of a name you'd rather use. With my mini book The Misleading Money Mantra, I used the 10 Problems model to point out 10 myths and lies that society says about money. When I finished, I went back through and renamed the titles to bate the reader into starting the chapter.

But if in doubt, clear wins over clever every time.

3 Sub-points Per Chapter

Once you've selected your outline format and the chapter topics, it's time to create your subtopic outline.

I start with 3 points per chapter and broke each of those into at least 3 smaller points (equalling 9 total for the chapter) and make those subheadings in the mini book. You can add extra if needed to organize information for the reader, but at least 3 big points and 3 smaller points for each of those breaks up the chapter into manageable chunks of information. If you aren't sure what sub-points to put in to support your chapter, you can always fall back on the things listed below to spark your creativity.

- Tips

- Steps

- Stories

- Things

- Secrets

- Benefits

- Lessons

- Reasons

- Mistakes

How much to Write Per Sub-point

I learned from Dickie Bush and Nicolas Cole in the Ship30 Writing Cohort, a great cadence and format you can create with your writing.

It is called 1-3-1. You write 1 opening sentence followed by a paragraph of 3 sentences. Then finish the section with a final sentence.

This section is 1-3-1 in practice.

As a starting point, I recommend you do at least two 1-3-1's for each of the 9 or more subpoints.

This will give the reader a good cadence for them to follow and gives you an idea of how tight you need to write your points. Depending on what outline model you choose will determine what your word count is at the end of your draft. You can add an additional 1-3-1 if you'd like, but that is your starting point.

Remember, a mini book is a highly consumable fast paced book that makes good on the promise to the reader with no fluff.

Editing Your Mini Book

Editing takes words thrown onto a page and makes it easy to read.

While getting your content into a manuscript is a huge win, it would embarrass most writers to release their rough draft into the world. If you feel that way, you are not alone! With mini books, you'll want to make sure your work doesn't have a lot of errors that will distract the reader so they can understand the points you are trying to make.

Along with reading through your draft and fixing the things you see, there are a few options you have with editing.

- Hiring an Editor
- Using Editing Tools

Using an Editor

Whether you have a family friend who will read through your manuscript or you are looking to throw down some money for a pro editor, this is a great way to make sure your manuscript is tight.

While I love editors, I do not hire one for every book or mini book I write. They can be expensive and often the good ones are booked out for months. I hate waiting months to get my manuscript back and the ones I've tried that were available on-demand, I'd rather they never touched my manuscript.

My point, if using an editor, get a good one.

Places to find an Editor

There are several marketplaces that you can find editors for your mini book.

- Fiverr

- Upwork

- Reedsy

Reedsy has the best quality of editors, but that also means they are more expensive and often booked out.

Editing Tools

Software-based editing tools are always available, really useful, and inexpensive.

I rely heavily on these tools to help me catch obvious misspellings, comma mistakes, and confusing sentences. These softwares even offer suggestions for rearranging sentences. For $25 a month or as little as $120 a year, you can have these editing tools available to you all the time.

The 2 primary options for editing tools are:

- ProWritingAid

- Grammarly

I use ProWritingAid because it helps me more, and is less expensive than Grammarly, but both are well worth the money when compared to hiring an editor.

For most people, I suggest using a software based editing tool instead of spending hundreds of dollars on an editor and having another reason to not release your mini book. If you use software based editing tools or hire an editor, make sure you and another person read your manuscript after completing the edit, looking for obvious errors and to do what is called a proofread. My wife and I team up to do the proofreading.

A great way to proofread is to read it out loud while recording an audiobook version of your book.

Chapter 5

When to Stop Writing a Mini Book

You are neck deep into your mini book and plowing into the topic when suddenly, you have a great idea.

This happens to most writers. We have self doubt about the work we are producing and imagine ways to "make it better." Typically, this means adding more stuff to the manuscript. I'm all for adding if it means fulfilling the promise to the reader or filling in a spot you forgot on your outline, but most new ideas we have are actually other mini book ideas.

Resist the urge to let the book slowly get bigger and bigger in scope.

In the tech space, this is called scope creep and it's procrastination in disguise. We do this because launching something you created into the world is scary. Your brain is afraid of you finishing the book and it not being good enough.

It feels safer to just keep working on it instead of taking the risk of letting others read it.

This is one of the biggest reasons I love mini books.

They ship fast. To keep you from scope creep, I've come up with a few rules that will serve as a straightjacket for you and for me. That way, we can stick to the plan and finish the mini book.

Sit still, this won't hurt a bit.

Wear the Mini Book Straight Jacket

You are a grown human being, so you can do what you want, but if you want a system to follow, here you go.

The mini book straight jacket has 3 rules:

1. **Tackle 1 Thing**

2. **Say it With Less**

3. **Leave Open Loops**

Let's review each rule.

1. Tackle 1 Thing

Mini books tackle one point, thoroughly.

Unlike writing about "How to Become an Insurance Adjuster" which tells you 500 different things, a mini book picks up one problem or thought, and says "what do I see?" Your point of view, the lens through which you see the world, is what makes the difference.

Never lose focus on the singular idea and never change your point of view.

2. Say It With Less

With a mini book, getting your point across fast with a punch is vital.

Long prose or drawn out stories don't fit with the cadence of a fast book. Filling your mini book with hooks, punches, and finishing lines that make a point clearly while entertaining makes writing more challenging.

Saying less is more and staying under 15,000 words is the sweet spot.

3. Leave Open Loops

While a cardinal sin in stand-alone legacy books is leaving open loops or unanswered questions, mini books do.

Because you are only tackling one question, you will accidentally or on purpose open up new thoughts, ideas, and questions with your point of view. You and the reader will think, "Well if that is true, what does that mean for XYZ?" That open loop is the next mini book(s) that you should write about or you can tackle if you decide to expand to a legacy non-fiction book.

Mini books are a form of idea and demand generation.

For example, if I suddenly dove into a complex Amazon ads strategy for mini books, this would be too far off my topic.

I'm here hoping to offer you an alternative to writing a full legacy non-fiction book, so you actually get it done. Any deviation from that central topic and goal is unnecessary. We answer the questions we need to, but leave the others open.

To summarize the mini book straight jacket,

- Tackle only one idea or question

- Say your point punchier with less words

- Create and leave open loops for the next book(s)

How You Know You Are Done

You may never feel done with your mini book, and that is OK.

There is always more to say and new ground to cover. The more you dive into your topic by writing a mini book, the more you'll realize you can explore and the more you learn. It's easy to keep pushing onto new ground and never finish.

Here are a few ways that you can know the writing is done and to put the pencil or keyboard down.

When You Hit Your Word Count

Once you've crossed the threshold of 5,000 words, you can say you've written enough for a mini book.

As I've said, staying under 15,000 should be your goal, so if you are approaching 15,000 words, you should be near completion. Word count is nothing more than that, a count. It doesn't factor in if the content is appropriate for the book, but it can guide you and let you know when your length has reached mini-book level.

This is your first signal to know that you can stop writing.

What If I Go Over the Word Count?

Going over 15,000 words is not the end of the world.

It could be a sign that you need to edit and remove some content, but not always. I dealt with this in my mini book, The Misleading Money Mantra. I was just under the word count on my first draft, but after adding references and quotes, it ballooned to over 1,000 words past it.

You can choose to leave your mini book longer than 15,000 words, but if you see anything that is unnecessary, be ruthless and remove it.

Above all, though, make sure you publish and don't use having "too many words" as an excuse to not share it with the world.

When You've Fulfilled Your Promise to the Reader

The most important measurement is seeing if you've kept your promise to the reader.

Read your title and subtitle. Did you fulfill that promise? If you haven't met the promise, you've got more writing to do. It doesn't matter if you are writing a tweet or an anthology, you must fulfill your promise to the reader.

This is your second guide to know that you are done writing.

When You've Finished Your Outline & Tackled the 1 Point

If you've completely filled in your outline, this is a signal that you are done writing.

You should also look at your topic and make sure you thoroughly tackled the one thing from all angles. You don't want the reader feeling like you dropped the ball halfway through a thought, but you don't want to go on side tangents. Stick to your outline and you'll be fine.

If you can check all three boxes, you'll know you can stop writing.

- Hit Your Word Count

- Fulfill the Promise to the Reader

- Finished Your Outline & Nailed the 1 Point

Chapter 6

Where to Publish and Promote Your Mini Book

When you've wrapped up your manuscript it's time to release your POV to the world.

For some, the aspect of publishing and promoting is more daunting than the process of writing. Don't worry it really isn't hard to get your book into the hands of readers. There are several easy options that will allow you to distribute worldwide without much of a fuss.

We'll look at the publishing and pricing options first and then dive into a few quick ways to promote your new mini book and find your first readers.

Mini Book Publishing Options

Having your mini book easily available for people to find is an important part of spreading the POV of your mini book.

Because this is a mini book we can immediately take off the table the option of publishing through a traditional publishing company. They are only interested in publishing books with around 30,000 words. This isn't all bad news.

There are still some great options for you to self-publish which means you'll get to keep the lion's share of any book royalties.

There are 3 types of publishing options I'll discuss here,

- **Website**

- **Aggregators**

- **Digital Book Stores**

Each one of these options is a great option for setting up distribution of your book.

We'll look at each one and the pros and cons.

Digital Book Stores

When self-publishing your own mini book, you can get your book for sale on all the major platforms or digital bookstores yourself.

- Amazon

- Barnes and Noble

- Kobo

- Apple

- Etc

Each of these have options where you can upload your manuscript, cover, book details, and set your pricing.

Within a few hours or days, you'll soon see your book for sale on their platform. Amazon is the leader in readers and book sales for self-published authors and where most authors start off publishing to. If you plan to do at least one digital book store, I'd recommend starting with Amazon.

Once you have your manuscript and cover, it takes less than a hour to upload your book to Amazon's KDP Publishing platform.

Aggregators

For most self-published authors, they have to decide, do I only publish to Amazon or publish to all the online bookstores?

If you publish to all of the bookstores, the industry says your book is "wide." You are casting a bigger net to catch more readers. This would take a fair amount of time if you have to track down all the platforms and upload your book and information to all of them.

Luckily, there are companies called aggregators that manage the distribution of your book to lots of platforms and bookstores at once.

Companies like,

- Draft2Digital

- Bookbaby

- Ingramspark

- PublishDrive

All will distribute to multiple digital store fronts.

For example, I use Draft2Digital and it distributes to 13+ digital book stores when I upload my book, cover, and details to it. If you decide to use an aggregator, I'd recommend uploading to Amazon yourself first. This gives you a little more control over your manuscript.

If you decide to make your book exclusive and only available on Amazon, they provide a few perks to authors.

Better royalty rates, additional marketing tools, and being included in the Kindle unlimited program are some of the benefits of being exclusive on Amazon. If you choose to enroll in their exclusive program, (called KDP Select) you have to sign up for 90 days at a time, but if you decide you want to go wide with an aggregator after your 90 days, you are free to do so. Even if you plan to go wide from the beginning, upload to Amazon separately and not use an aggregator to distribute to Amazon.

Just trust me on this one.

Author Website

You don't have to upload your mini book to any digital bookstore, you can create your own.

You can sell your mini book directly to readers on your own website. There are many tools that make this possible, but at the time of this writing, Gumroad is the simplest, most cost effective, and easiest to use. And you can choose to do both digital bookstores and sell it on your own website.

This gives you both lots of control and distribution for those searching on those platforms.

Pricing Your Mini Book to Sell

It's your book so you determine the price, but what your price should be is determined by a few factors.

- Your strategy

- How big is the problem you solve?

- How many other books/solutions are there for this problem?

How Big is the Problem?

Your problem or question you tackle in your mini book will ultimately dictate how much you can charge for your book.

If you are solving a problem of "How to Bake Cookies", there are hundreds if not thousands of sources telling you how to bake cookies, and readers will not be as likely to pay more for your book than the rest of the market. If you are solving the problem of "How to Bake Cookies for a Diabetic Vegan" you could charge more! It's now a bigger problem and harder to find a solution for the topic.

The more different and interesting your POV is, the more readers will pay for your mini book.

The brain surgeon who writes a mini book about a breakthrough technique is going to demand a much higher price from the market for his mini book than the baking example. How much money or value is your solution going to bring the reader? How much impact will this have on their lives?

These are some questions you must ask yourself when determining the pricing of your mini book.

Your Strategy

Your strategy behind why you wrote your mini book can help you determine your price as well.

If you are trying to reach as many people as possible about with a wide reaching topic, a lower price between $0.99 - $4.99 would make sense. If your audience is a mini niche and you have an interesting POV, you may want to charge $9.99 to $99.99 depending on the topic.

There are even strategies when $0.00 is the right price.

It's up to you to decide what you want to do with your mini book.

If this is your first digital product and you are nervous. I recommend starting between $.99 - $4.99. The goal is to get your first sales, reviews, and fans. You can raise your price at a later date, but getting some quick wins in will give you tremendous momentum and feedback from your readers.

Don't overthink this, just get it done and get it for sale.

Ways to Promote Your Mini Book

One of the biggest fears of all authors is that they'll write a book and no one will want to read it.

This is a legitimate fear. Often authors write in a backroom and tell few people about what they are working on. They come up with a topic on their own and spend months or years writing a legacy non-fiction book, only to find out it wasn't what readers were looking for.

I believe in validating your idea before you ever write your first word.

This is also the beginning of promoting your book.

You can use social media platforms or real-life interactions with people to see if your book would resonate with them. I believe that social validation through social media is a great way to test ideas with small posts, tweets, and content. The internet is anonymous and you'll see what people really think or if they don't care.

If no one is responding to your content and topic, you may not have found a good way to talk about.

This stops many would be authors from ever writing and I hate that.

Authors get discouraged because they just want to write. If that is you, screw social media and write what you want to write. Just realize that the book is for you and as Nicolas Cole of Ship30for30 says, "Don't be shocked if no one wants to buy your book because you wrote it for you."

The point is, promotion takes place before, during, and after the writing of your mini book.

Let's look at some promotion strategies for your new mini book.

Attention Generation

This is the most effective strategy for any author to promote their mini book or legacy non-fiction book, but it also takes work.

Attention generation is where you go to the public and provide content about your topic, which generates attention for you and eventually your mini book. Some call this "content creation" but it isn't just about creating content. It's about getting someone's attention for the right reasons.

Once you have someone's attention in the right frame of mind, you can build trust and eventually earn a customer.

There are many ways you can execute attention generation,

- Podcasts

- Speaking

- Social Media Posts

Most authors will need to start with social media posts to generate enough attention to get podcast interviews or speaker engagements lined up.

Writing every day on LinkedIn, Twitter, Medium, Facebook, or other platforms is one of the best ways to generate an audience and attention. With the virality of these platforms, it only takes one post going viral to generate enough attention to make a big difference.

If you need help learning how to write and publish digital writing every day on these platforms, check out the Ship30for30 Writing Cohort by Nicolas Cole and Dickie Bush.

By providing useful and relevant content to your niche about the topic of your mini book you will naturally find customers wanting your book. It can take time, so don't get discouraged if the first hundred times you post you don't go viral or get book sales. It doesn't take going viral to sell a book.

It just takes one person who needs help solving the problem your mini book addresses.

One of the best things about this strategy is you can use it to build your social following and turn that social following into email subscribers. You can use your mini book as a free gift for people joining your mailing list or just give a big takeaway, summary, snippet, or listicle PDF that is on the topic of your book. Growing your email list in one of the best ways to sell a future mini book so if you have plans for more products or more mini books, giving away the first one can be a great strategy for growing your email list.

Your mini book can be the foundation of your social content, lead magnet (free gift), product, and business.

Aren't mini books great?

Book Promotion Sites

What's better than being able to email your list about your book?

Being able to email other people's list about your book! There are book deal websites that do nothing but collect readers who are looking for book deals and tell them books that are a bargain. You can purchase a spot on those emails and promote your book to readers interested in your genre and topic.

There are millions of readers are on these lists.

Some of the book promotion websites are,

- ENT

- Bookbub

- Book Raid

- EReaderIQ

- Robin Reads

- Fussy Librarian

- Free Kindle Books

- Freebooksy/Bargain Booksy

Typically, you'll pay $20 - $100 to be listed in one of their daily emails.

There are upsides and downsides to using book promo sites.

Pro's

- Bump in Sales

- Massive Audience

- Get readers into Your Series

- Get Reviews for Your Books

- Higher ranking on Amazon/Bookstores

Con's

- Readers are Deal Seekers

- Book Must Be Discounted or Free

- Not All Promo Sites Get the Same Results for all Topics

- Some Sites Don't Accept Mini Books (under 100 pages)

This strategy works best if you are planning on Amazon or other bookstores being a big part of your long-term sales and credibility strategy or if you plan on writing multiple books in a series.

I generated over 300 reviews for my book God is Like a Geyser, only using promo sites to find readers. This gives my book and series credibility compared to the 20 or 30 reviews I started with.

Book promo site email subscribers are readers. It is likely they will at least attempt to read your book and as a result many will leave a review.

Paid Ads

My least recommended strategy, but still viable for mini books, is paid ads.

You can purchase ads on many of the social media platforms, book stores, Google, websites, or the leading book promotion site, Bookbub, to drive customers to your mini book. If you are so inclined to try paid ads, I'd stick to trying out Facebook, Amazon ads, or Bookbub ads to start.

You can blow through a lot of money in a hurry if you aren't careful, so any testing you do make sure it is a small amount per day.

This is another strategy that works better if you have other products or books in your series because you can sell a book at low cost or lose money on your initial ads but still be profitable long term.

Out of the platforms listed, I've had the most success with Bookbub ads.

Chapter 7

Final Thoughts

Alright, you now know enough to write and publish a mini book.

The only question is, why are you still reading this book? The world needs your point of view. Someone out there has a problem and you are the only person who can solve it. This is a powerful and exciting call, but one that can be overwhelming.

I hope I've removed the burden of word count and set you free to create the work that you've kept bottled up inside you.

It's time for you to write a mini book, right after you leave me an honest review of this one.

Reviews are the only way others know if this book is worth their time and money. It'd mean the world if you'd take a minute and share your thoughts with the world. You can leave a review on your device or digital book store or head to https://minibookmodel.com/ and click "Leave a Review".

It's Time to Fire Up Your Engine

You've built your chassis:

Your niche
Your problem
Your strategy.

That was Stage 1.

Now it's time for Stage 2: **build the engine**. Yeah I know I gave you a brief overview of my outline and structure, but people kept asking me "how do I actually write the book?"

So I'll guide you step by step.

The Mini Book you're about to write is more than content, it's the core asset that drives your authority and your revenue. And don't worry: you don't have to be a "real writer" to do it.

The next book in this series, **Mini Book Writing**, will walk you step-by-step through outlining, drafting, and finishing your book fast. No fluff. No writer's block. Just a framework and instruction that gets it done.

You've got your chassis. Now it's time to bolt in the engine.

Grab Mini Book Writing and let's build something powerful.

- Chris Stanley

P.S. I included a free preview for you of Mini Book Writing in the next few pages. If you want to contact me email me at Chris@chris-stanley.com or connect with me on LinkedIn.

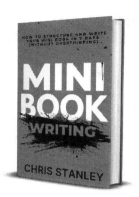

BONUS: How to Complete Your Own Mini Book

Ready to publish your mini book with confidence? The Mini Book Success Checklist is your step-by-step guide to making it happen. (inclues bonus resources for every step!)

Here's what you'll find inside:

- Prepping Guide: Craft a compelling title, subtitle, and outline that capture your readers' attention.

- Penning Checklist: Break down your book into manageable chapters and sections, ensuring smooth and efficient writing.

- Publishing Blueprint: Get your book formatted, uploaded, and ready for sale with ease.

- Promotion Plan: Learn the key strategies to launch your book, attract readers, and gain reviews.

- Downloadable Printer Friendly PDF (with checkable boxes)

- Notion checklist (for those who love staying organized in Notion software)

Head to MiniBookModel.com

Mini Book Writing

You've built your chassis:

Your niche

Your problem
Your strategy.

That was Stage 1.

Now it's time for Stage 2: **build the engine**. Yeah I know I gave you a brief overview of my outline and structure, but people kept asking me "how do I actually write the book?"

So I'll guide you step by step.

The Mini Book you're about to write is more than content, it's the core asset that drives your authority and your revenue. And don't worry: you don't have to be a "real writer" to do it.

The next book in this series, **Mini Book Writing**, will walk you step-by-step through outlining, drafting, and finishing your book fast. No fluff. No writer's block. Just a framework and instruction that gets it done.

You've got your chassis. Now it's time to bolt in the engine.

Grab Mini Book Writing and let's build something powerful.

P.S. I included a free preview for you of that back in the next few pages.

HOW TO STRUCTURE AND WRITE YOUR MINI BOOK IN 7 DAYS (WITHOUT OVERTHINKING)

MINI BOOK WRITING

CHRIS STANLEY

Introduction to the Mini Book Writing (Preview)

I've written and published over 25 books.

These books have laid the foundation for my online businesses and presence. I am not an "intellectual," in fact, I'm a college dropout. I live on a sailboat with my wife and kids, traveling the world all thanks to the books I've written and the customers I have found because of those books.

It all started with one book.

You've heard "writing a book is so hard and takes months or years."

Yes, it's true, writing a book is a mental challenge. But it isn't complicated to write a book. You just need to know what to do.

Then sit down and actually do it.

I've seen the mental challenge get to my own mini book coaching clients as they get stuck in their own head.

I created this book because I hated seeing them face the blank page. Faced with a mountain of experience and knowledge, they feel unsure how to mine through it and find the gold to offer to their readers. I wanted to give them and you, a structure so tight that you could know exactly what sentence you needed to write next.

That is why I created the Mini Book Writing. (originally published as Mini Book Straitjacket for reasons you'll see soon)

No more guessing at how to write a book.

You no longer have to fear starting your book, paralyzed by the thought of getting stuck and not knowing how to write the next chapter or section. This book will guide you through everything from choosing a title that hooks your reader, creating an outline that will guide your reader, all the way to completing your first draft of your manuscript. This book will teach you to write nonfiction books that are around 10,000 – 15,000 words long.

I call these, mini books.

These are the steps this book will take you through:

- Creating a POWER promise that causes someone to want to buy your book

- Choosing an outline structure that will make it easy for you to fill in the chapter titles without stressing out

- Establishing key points for each chapter of your book without chasing bunny trails

- Building a mental scaffolding for your reader that makes it easy for them to follow

- Knowing what to write each and every sentence of your entire book

- Virtual guaranteeing you'll finish your book once you start it

- Completing the book to include things like lead magnets so you can turn readers into leads

Each chapter of this book will guide you through a step of the journey.

In these chapters, I have broken down the process of writing a non-fiction book to make it as simple as a color-by-number activity. At the end of each chapter, I will give you an action step that you'll need to take to create your book. I recommend you read a chapter of this book, then put it down and go do what it tells you.

Your journey to becoming a best-selling published author starts now.

Turn the page, take action, and see your mini book turn from an idea into reality.

Author's Note

I wrote this book in 6 days.

The day I came up with the idea for this book I knew I was in trouble. I'd have to write it starting that day and finish it within 7 days. Otherwise I'd be a fraud and this book could lose credibility.

So I decided to write it publicly in less than 7 days.

Each day I posted to my social media and newsletter followers updates on the book and the chapter(s) that I wrote.

After I I finished the book I went back and did an edit and some updates, but the first draft is over 90% still in tact from 6 days of work. I spent 2-3 hours a day and a total of 15 hours between outlining and writing the 13,500+ words in this book. I still was the CEO of my company, had webinars, and was moving my families sailboat for 10ish hours a day.

I followed the model I'm teaching you in this book to write this book you have in your hand to prove to you that it can be done.

Step 1: Create a POWER Promise to the Reader (Preview)

The number one thing you can do to make your book successful is to make a strong promise to your reader.

This promise to the reader is a promise of what problem you are going to help them solve. This promise is made through your title, your subtitle, and your book cover. The reader will often decide on purchasing and reading your book based on these three things alone.

The success of your book is determined long before you write your first word; it's decided when you choose a problem and make a promise.

You communicate your promise in 5 different ways:

- **P** – Problem the reader faces.

- **O** – Offer of the solution to the problem.

- **W** – Words that create a great hook in your title.

- **E** – Expectation of transformation stated in the subtitle.

- **R** – Reveal the genre and overall theme with your cover.

We'll break each of these down.

Problem & Offer of a Solution

Every good business and every good book starts by solving the correct problem for the customer.

When starting a business, you must know your customer and then decide what problem you want to solve for that customer. This is no different with your books. Each mini book you write should solve one singular problem your customer has.

It should help them achieve the big promise that your company aims to fulfill.

For instance, I help people write mini books, and this book is helping with the problem of knowing how to get your first draft done.

Choosing a Problem

If you are having trouble choosing what problem to solve, consider these 3 growth catalysts:

1. **Bigger is better:** The bigger the problem or the pool of people that have a problem, the better.

2. **Smaller is faster:** A smaller promise that is quicker to experience makes the reader have a fast win and causes good reviews and viral word of mouth.

3. **First in series bonus:** If the problem you help solve is the first problem they will encounter, they will come back to you for additional answers.

The more of the growth catalysts your problem has, the better for your book and business. (You can find more on this concept in my book Simple Online Business Model.)

Choosing a Solution

Your answer to the problem doubles as the category of your solution.

You can solve a problem in several different ways, but how you choose to solve that problem defines your category of solution and book. To get a book written without taking a lot of your time, you could hire a ghostwriter, use ChatGPT, or write a mini book. My solution and therefore category is mini books.

Your solution is very important because it speaks a lot about the content of the book.

If you are having trouble knowing what solution or category your book should fall into, you may be trying to write the wrong book. The problem you are helping someone solve should be one you've already solved yourself. Then, the solution and category you are writing about should be the way that you solved that problem!

This is how you take the mystery out of writing a non-fiction book because the book will practically write itself if you are just telling someone how you solved a problem in the past with a particular solution.

Timeline

Determine how soon the reader can expect their problem to be solved with your solution.

Going back to the "smaller is faster" point, it is easier to sell a book on how to write a non-fiction book in 7 days compared to how to spend 2 years writing your next book. You'll want to set realistic expectations and have real-world experience showing that their problem can be solved or at least begin to be solved in the amount of time you promise. Look back through your journey and see how fast you solved it. If someone else you know solved it quicker, then look at why and try to incorporate how they got faster results into your book.

Determining how fast someone can accomplish this, along with the problem and category of solution, will prepare you to come up with a killer title and subtitle in the next section of this chapter.

Title & Subtitle (Words & Expectation)

Title

A good title is the hook of your book.

Think of some of the greatest books of all time: Tipping Point, Snow Leopard, Start With Why. Each of these titles drives your curiosity and pulls you in, making you want to know more. Just like a good copywriter knows that a headline makes a sales page or that a headline can make an ad, the hook of the book—your title—can make or break the book.

This is why I believe you must start with the title & subtitle before you ever type a single word.

Having a good hook or a good title can actually birth a book all by itself.

I've written several books that were inspired by simply coming up with a hook. My books PDR Cash Box, Simple Online Business Model, and Misleading Money Mantra all began because I stumbled across these titles or hooks. This proves that the title is more than just a title; it's a hook for the reader and a hook for the author.

You will find it much easier to write a book when you are captivated by the title.

3 Different Types of Titles

There are 3 common types of titles I see expert-based nonfiction books utilize:

1. **One Word Titles:** Examples include Ask by Ryan Levesque, Blink by Malcolm Gladwell, and Margin by Richard Swenson.

2. **Framework Titles:** Examples include 4-Hour Workweek by Tim Ferriss, Simple Online Business Model by yours truly, and Atomic Habits by James Clear. These use the name

of the core concept or framework as the title.

3. **Brand Titles:** Examples include Business Made Simple by Donald Miller, Rich Dad Poor Dad by Robert Kiyosaki, and the IA Path Playbooks. These titles establish a company name in readers' minds.

Picking which of these to use will eliminate the name overwhelm many first-time authors face.

(Framework titles can be an awesome launching point for a new business or a new product. If you don't have your own framework, you can easily create one based on the topic you're looking to write a book on. Download my FRAMEworks worksheet to create your own at Minibookstraitjacket.com.)

Subtitle

While the title, as a hook, can be vague, the subtitle must be clear.

This is where you clear up any confusion or ambiguity in your one-word title. Even with framework titles like Simple Online Business Model, you need to clarify what will happen when your framework is applied. The reader wants to know: if I read the book and apply your framework, what will happen?

This is the job of your subtitle, to eliminate any questions that remain after the title.

The ambiguous one-word titles become perfectly clear when you add the subtitle:

- Ask: The Counterintuitive Online Method to Discover Exactly What Your Customers Want to Buy . . . Create a Mass of Raving Fans . . . and Take Any Business to the Next Level

- Blink: The Power of Thinking Without Thinking

- Margin: Restoring Emotional, Physical, Financial, and Time Reserves to Overloaded Lives

You might have been unsure what you'd get out of "Ask," but now you know exactly what the author is promising.

Our framework and brand titles zero in on the transformation someone will experience if they apply their framework:

- The 4-Hour Workweek: Escape the 9-5, Live Anywhere, and Join the New Rich

- Atomic Habits: An Easy & Proven Way to Build Good Habits & Break Bad Ones

- Business Made Simple: 60 Days to Master Leadership, Sales, Marketing, Execution, Management, Personal Productivity, and More

A good subtitle offers a clear transformation that the reader will experience if they pick up, read, and apply your book.

Cover

Your book cover reveals to the reader the genre, theme, and feel of the book.

Is it going to be a female power book? Or a book written by a manly man like Bear Grylls? Is it an intellectual or a straightforward how-to book?

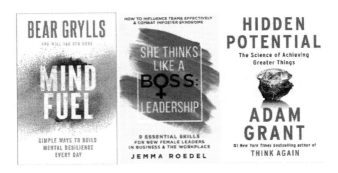

Letting the potential reader know will help them decide if this is the right fit for them, which increases the number of happy readers and the average rating of your review.

My framework for creating book covers is the QUICK Book Cover Model:

- **Q** – Qualify what a good selling book cover looks like by finding three you like the feel of on Amazon.

- **U** – Upload those designs to Canva or Bookbrush.

- **I** – Insert the elements and recreate the book cover as close as possible.

- **C** – Customize the cover by changing the title, subtitle, author name, images, and colors to match your book and brand.

- **K** – Kindle ready, ensure your cover meets Kindle requirements and is ready for publication.

Let's run through these quickly.

Q – Qualify a Best Selling Book Cover

Head to Amazon and search the non-fiction best selling books in a broad category like business or self-help, that will match the big category of your book.

Find three books with hundreds if not thousands of reviews. These will serve as your bestselling models. Find titles that have similar number of words as your title.

Once you find a title that you feel you'd like the look and feel of something similar, right-click and save it to your computer.

U – Upload Designs to Canva/BookBrush

Take your three designs and upload them to your design software of choice, something like Canva or Bookbrush.

You're going to select an ebook cover as the template and dimensions. You'll use each of these designs you've downloaded as the background of your design. Simply lock it in place so you can manipulate things on top of it without moving it around.

This will serve as something you can model after.

I – Insert Elements

You'll add text and images to recreate the book cover.

You'll need to determine the style and size of the font. Match the colors on the background, images, and text. Find images that match any on the cover.

Most book covers are simpler than you first imagine, so get it really close to the original, but don't stress if it's a little off.

C – Customize the Cover

Now you change everything to make it your book.

Change the words to be your title, subtitle, and author name. Change the images to be your own unique ones. Change the colors to match your brand and vibe.

In the end, you'll have something that you drew inspiration from but doesn't look exactly like the original cover, like the ones I did for my friend Jeff below.

Inspiration   Result

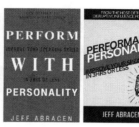

K – Kindle (KDP) Ready

You'll need to make sure your cover is ready to upload to Amazon's publishing service called KDP:

- 1,600 x 2,560 pixels

- Under 50 MB

- JPEG file type

Download your file, make sure it meets those requirements, and you have your book cover DONE!

You now have a POWER promise to your reader.

You are hooking the potential reader with your title, communicating a clear transformation they will experience if they buy, read, and apply your book. Plus, you have a cover that communicates all of that and the theme and feel of your book in an instant. Your reader has no questions remaining about what you are offering.

This POWER promise guide you every step through the rest of your book creation journey.

Action Step: Craft Your POWER Promise

1. **P** – Identify the problem the reader faces. Write down this problem clearly and concisely.

2. **O** – Determine the offer of a solution you are providing to solve this problem. Make sure your offer is compelling and actionable.

3. **W** – Find the words that will create a great hook for your title.

4. **E** – Set the expectation of transformation by stating it with a clear subtitle.

5. **R** – Reveal the genre and overall theme by creating your book cover.

By completing these steps, you'll have a strong POWER promise that hooks your readers and sets clear expectations, making your book more attractive and compelling. Share your progress with the Mini Book Masters community to get feedback and refine your promise even further.

You can also email me at Chris@Chris-Stanley.com your POWER promise and cover. I'd love to see it.

Step 2: Choose Your Book Outline (Preview)

Your outline of the mini book puts restrictions on you.

It forces you to fit your topic and book into a tight structure. Embracing restrictions is what makes the Mini Book Straitjacket work. It allows you to quit thinking about all the possibilities and focus in on just the next point, sub-point, and eventually sentence.

Often we avoid simple outlines because it doesn't feel "smart," but clear outlines are the easiest and simplest way to start and easier for the reader to follow along.

Here are the three outlines I restrict myself to using.

- W's

- Sequential

- 10 Problems

Let's look at each outline individually and see when one is better than the other.

W's Outline

The W's Outline (technically the 5W1H Method... but that is a mouthful) forces you to ask the key questions about a topic.

- What

- Who

- Why

- When

- Where

- How

Asking these questions about your topic will force you to explain your topic from all the most commonly asked questions.

Best Used for Concepts

When you want to introduce a new concept to readers, the W's method is king.

In the Mini Book Model, I used the W's method to introduce the concept of mini books. By using the W's method, I was able to thoroughly explain and give a broad overview and introduction to the topic. This outline lays the foundation for something that people are not familiar with.

This may be the simplest of all the outlines, but don't let its simplicity make you think it's not useful.

Here are some concept legacy non-fiction books,

- "Thinking, Fast and Slow" by Daniel Kahneman

- "The Power of Habit" by Charles Duhigg

- "Grit: The Power of Passion and Perseverance" by Angela Duckworth

To write a book on a concept, use the W's model and apply the Mini Book Straitjacket.

Keep It Obvious

When using the W's outline, keep your questions simple and obvious.

Don't try and dive deep into "What questions should I ask?" You aren't trying to outsmart the reader. You are trying to meet the reader exactly where they are. They have questions and you want to show you have answers.

Here is an example of a simple, obvious outline from my book Mini Book Model.

- <u>What </u>I Mean When I Say Mini Book

- <u>Who </u>Writes and Who Reads Mini Books

- <u>Why </u>You Should Write a Mini Book

- <u>How </u>You Write a Mini Book

- <u>When</u> to Stop Writing a Mini Book

- <u>Where</u> to Publish and Promote Your Mini Book

These questions made it super easy for me to sit down and answer the obvious questions and readers loved it.

Renaming Your Chapter Titles

Maybe you don't want to be seen as a simpleton.

You may feel self-conscious about writing chapter titles with all W's (and 1 H). You can rename your chapter title to "hide" the fact that you are using a W's model. I recommend you only rename after your writing is complete.

If you start off trying to get fancy and clever, you may never start writing.

Here is an example of my Mini Book Model chapters redone to hide the W's outline.

- Understanding the Concept of a Mini Book

- The Audience: Writers and Readers of Mini Books

- The Benefits of Writing a Mini Book

- Steps to Crafting a Mini Book

- Knowing When Your Mini Book is Complete

- Effective Platforms for Publishing and Promoting Your Mini Book

To use this outline, just write down the W's and fill in the blank for your topic.

Sequential Outline

The sequential outline walks someone through how to do something, start to finish.

This type of outline works best with processes. Want to teach someone how to build their first raised bed garden? How to build a marketing funnel in ClickFunnels?

Perfect, use the sequential outline.

Roadmaps

Most businesses have a journey they want their customers to go on.

What better way to explain the steps that your ideal customer should take to solve their problems than with a roadmap laid out in a mini book? My best-selling book in my insurance adjuster series, Independent Adjuster's Playbook, gave readers a 7-step roadmap to follow. It showed them what to do at each step if they wanted to become an independent adjuster.

This book sold my high-end coaching services for years and still helps me land new clients today.

Here is the roadmap that book was written off of.

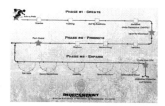

With a roadmap book, you guide your potential clients on how to achieve the results they want on their own.

Then you have the chance to tastefully tell them if they need help with any step of the journey that you have a solution to that. It is a great type of outline to build a funnel of prospects coming your way. If you have a roadmap for your customers, those steps serve as the chapter titles for your book.

This book you are reading... is a Sequential Outline.

Framework

If you have a signature framework, a sequential book is also a perfect outline.

When I wrote the Simple Online Business Model, I used my acronym "SIMPLE" to guide the outline. By narrowing down to just the most basic elements, you avoid the overwhelm of endless possibilities and can maintain a clear focus. This structure not only simplifies your writing process but also makes the reader's experience smooth by making the content easier to follow.

If you have a way to do something but you want it to be a framework, here is how I turn any process into a framework.

- F - Formulate a process

- R - Refine into simple steps

- A - Account for the number of steps

- M - Make an Acronym

- E - Explain with a Visual

Then if your FRAME actually "works," you have a framework you can build your book around.

Business Flywheel

I found that a sequential outline works really well for laying a foundation for the future.

Not only do you provide your readers and potential customers with a clear process to follow, but you also establish your credibility as an authority on the topic while presenting the easy onboarding ramp for coaching, courses, or even other books that you can mention in your book. I ended up writing a book for nearly every step of my insurance adjuster roadmap as well as corresponding courses.

By looking at your roadmap, you can see where people are getting stuck and create content, posts, books, courses, or coaching programs for those specific steps.

This clarity is not only good for your reader but a breakthrough for you.

You clear the confusion in your mind and identify a path to guide your customer through each step of their journey. You no longer have to wonder issues your customers have. You can stop guessing what hurdles your customers face. Look at your roadmap, see where people are getting stuck, and create content, posts, books, courses, or coaching programs for those steps.

This creates a flywheel in your business with your roadmap book acting as the flagship to promote them all.

10 Problems Outline

The 10 Problems outline focuses on your readers' biggest obstacles.

You determine what is holding them back from getting the result they desire and help smash those obstacles. If you've been in your industry for a decent amount of time, you can likely identify the biggest things holding people back from having success. 10 Problems Outlines work great if you are writing about a mindset shift or wanting to zero in on challenges they are facing.

All you do is list the problems out and that is your topic for each chapter.

Pain Points

The 10 Problems Outline centers around the pain points of your customer, which is usually a really good idea.

It zeroes in on what is ailing the customer and offers a solution, making your book an easy buy for a reader. If they suffer from one of the problems, they'll buy your book. I used the 10 Problems Outline in my mini book, Misleading Money Mantra: How Chasing Money Is Holding You Back From the Life and Business of Your Dreams. I listed the 10 big misconceptions and lies society was pushing on people and offered a solution to being a slave to money.

You can write a book about the pain points of sprinklers, writing a book, or any topic you choose.

Most Popular

The biggest problem you'll run into is which problems to tackle.

You'll likely have a long list. But if you are having trouble coming up with a list of problems, go online to groups that discuss your topic. I'm sure you'll find people complaining about your industry and what's wrong with it.

Write down every problem you see and can think of.

If you have more than 10, congratulations. You can trim it down by focusing on the most popular. If you aren't sure which problems are the most popular, you can use a Google Analytics Keyword analyzer to see how many times people search for solving that problem in Google.

That'll give you a great idea of which problems are affecting the most people.

Making It Feel Good

Here is the problem with the 10 Problems Outline.

Your reader doesn't want to read a bunch of problems. Your reader wants to have solutions to their problems. Once you have a list of problems, you'll want to reword them into solutions.

When the reader encounters your book, they'll see an ocean of peace because you offer so many solutions to their biggest problems.

This transformation from problems to solutions will make your book more appealing and provide a sense of hope and progress to your readers. It also positions you as the doctor to their ailments. This does great at establishing a deeper relationship with the reader.

They'll want to visit you the next time they have an ailment of any kind around your topic. It'll work on turning them from a reader to a customer.

Action Step: Create Your Mini Book Outline

1. Decide whether the W's Outline, Sequential Outline, or 10 Problems Outline best fits your topic and goals.

   a. Remember to focus on what will make your content most accessible and valuable to your readers.

   b. Consider: are you writing about a Concept (W's), a Process (Sequential), or Mindset Shift (10 Problems)

2. **Draft Your Outline:**
   Spend the next 30 minutes drafting an outline for your mini book using the chosen structure.

Keep it simple and straightforward, focusing on the chapter titles only at this point.

3. **Share Your Outline:**

Post your outline in the comments of this post or the Mini Book Masters Community at MiniBook.news for feedback and support.

By taking this action step, you'll be well on your way to creating a focused and effective mini book that resonates with your readers. Embrace the structure, and let it guide you to success!

I hope you enjoyed this sample of the Mini Book Straitjacket. If you'd like to read the entire book head to MiniBookStraitjacket.com

SIMPLE

ONLINE BUSINESS MODEL

FIND YOUR NICHE AND MAKE MONEY IN YOUR SPARE TIME

CHRIS STANLEY

Introduction to the Simple Online Business Model (Sample)

For the last seven years, I've been living the American dream. I'm writing on the deck of my sailboat, flanked on either side by twinkling waves. I enjoy the view of other boats floating in the distance, knowing that my business—now just shy of seven figures per year—practically runs itself. I can work from anywhere and do what I want, when I want.

How did I get there?

Since you picked up this book, I guess that's what you're asking. I didn't do anything radical. In fact, I believe you can achieve online business success as well. And I'm going to help you.

Your biggest enemy is information overload. Thousands of marketers vie for your attention, torpedoing you with mind-numbing online business strategies. I've tried most of them. Looking back at what has worked and hasn't, I realize I overcomplicated stuff.

I needed to simplify the way I thought about my business and remove distractions. I had to boil down business concepts to make them simple and easy to remember. That's how I came up with a super SIMPLE business framework—a six-step roadmap for anyone running or starting an online business.

Here's the outline:

S – **S**elect Your Niche
I – **I**nvestigate It Daily
M – **M**arket Your Expertise
P – **P**ackage Your Knowledge
L – **L**everage Your Email List
E – **E**ducate Your Customers With Digital Products & Services

The steps follow the order in which you run your business, whether that's a startup or a running company. It works for the smallest niches as well as mega categories, and you can use any marketing tactic you want—from marketing funnels and text messaging to backflips and kickflips. They'll all fit under one of the six steps.

You can make your business as complicated as you want within each of these steps, but I promise this is all you need to start and maintain your business. It doesn't *need* to be complicated.

In the chapters ahead, we'll silence all noise about running a business. Each breaks down one bucket of the SIMPLE Online Business Model. At the end of each chapter, I'll show you how to implement it.

My online business has changed my life. I live on a sailboat with my wife and three kids, traveling full time. When tired of the water, we take our converted school bus west to Yellowstone and other US national parks.

This was our dream. And our online business, along with God's blessing, made it possible.

Whatever your reasons for wanting a change, I'm sure you can grow a successful business *and* have a healthy family—if you build a SIMPLE Online Business.

Let's get started.

S - Select a Niche (Sample)

When I started my online business, I was struggling. My problem was that I had no idea who I was serving or what I was talking about. What type of business was I running anyway?

I made a classic beginner's mistake. I should have chosen my ideal customer before anything else. Once I figured out who my customers were, I could discover their problem and help them solve it.

These three things put together, create your niche.

That is all a business is, a problem solver. And to choose the kind of problem you can solve, you must start with the customer.

Your Customer

You can get super complicated in picking your ideal customer, also called your customer avatar, but let's go simple.

There are only three people you can serve.

"But Chris, there are eight billion people on the planet!"

Yes, but for your online business, there are only three that you have to choose from.

You can serve:

- Who you are

- Who you were

- Who you love

This choice will shape your business.

If you want to serve the you of today (a thirty-year-old entrepreneur), your business will look different than if you serve the you of back in college. And even more different if you choose "who you love" and decide it is your eighty-year-old grandma Ethel.

Each option has advantages and disadvantages, so let's look at them one by one.

Who You Are

The easiest person to relate to is someone like you. You know what they're thinking. You know what they're asking. You get them.

So, choosing "who you are" as your ideal customer has a lot of advantages. To serve this customer, all you must do is learn something new. You can decide today to serve someone of your competency level and become a master at the things they *wish* they knew.

But here's the drawback: you can't rely on what you already know—because your customer likely already knows it as well.

This is why many people believe you should choose option 2.

Who You Were

Imagine having a beer with your college-age self. What would you tell him? You have a ton of experience and business expertise to pass on. You're ahead of him. You can offer him the winning numbers for the upcoming lottery of life.

For that reason, "who you were" is the most popular choice for an ideal customer.

You don't have to learn anything new to get started. You just share what you know. When I started my online business, I had been an independent auto insurance adjuster for seven years. One day, I showed up on LinkedIn and began posting about winning in my industry.

Those behind me on the journey loved it, and my peers sent new people my way.

Nicolas Cole, a popular digital writing teacher, suggests you use the two-year test when writing. Who were you two years ago? Help that person. Two years is close enough for you to remember what happened. And your skills have had enough time to become helpful to that person.

Who You Love

While options one and two are simple, you may not like either. You might want to serve Grandma Ethel and her bingo club. Or a generation of children in the same phase as your kids. Perhaps you have such a heart for a group of people that you *have* to serve them.

Great, then you choose "who you love."

You're passionate about them, and that's an advantage. But you don't know them as well as yourself. This ideal customer requires more research, guessing, and trial and error. So, it will take you much longer than the "who you are" or "who you were" customer avatars.

Their Problem

Once you've defined your customer, you must locate a problem she's facing. You could help Grandma Ethel with her knitting, find her a date at eighty, or prevent her from getting scammed.

If you aren't sure what problems to solve or are overwhelmed with the number of them, I've got three growth catalysts for you to consider.

Bigger is Better

The bigger your customer's problem, the better. Massive problems reap massive appreciation when solved—and that means more $$$. So, a careful assessment is a must. If we slack, we might select a problem that doesn't mean much to our customers, and we'll be stuck with an empty bank account.

Helping a couple save their marriage is an example of a big problem. People will pay big money for your solution. On the other hand, the issue of fingernail clippers not cutting straight is small and will never get you the same kind of money.

But atomic problems like that can earn you a good buck, too. In such a case, it is the pool of customers that needs to be big. You're not likely to find people willing to spend $3,000 on a nail clipper, but if you can relieve six hundred people of crooked toenails for $5 each, you're doing just as well.

"Bigger is better" is a creed to remember.

Smaller is Faster

Small tasks are delivered faster. Teaching someone to fix her résumé is much easier than saving her marriage. A resume is updated immediately, and your customers will send out job applications the same day. But it may take months or years to know whether you've helped save a marriage.

Start out with a problem that is annoying but speedily solved. You will have a higher likelihood of success.

First in Series Bonus

If you solve someone's first problem, this customer will likely return to you. For example, if you help a couple get their first date, you can also help them decide if they should marry. Then, you can help them with their wedding planning, child-rearing, marriage counseling, and other relationship advice.

This is an exponential bonus, an unfair advantage in business.

If you have to choose between two problems and one is first in a series of problems, then I'd lean toward the first one.

Your Solution (or Category)

You chose your ideal customer and his problem. Now, you need to figure out how you think that you can solve it.

The key here is to find what direction you are heading. What category of solution you are pointing people to, not a product, that comes later. If your customer's problem is his girlfriend not liking his beard, you could help him with different types of solutions.

- Shaving

- Electrolysis

- Relationships Advice (finding a girlfriend that likes your beard)

So what do you think your solution and category is? Which one?

There are often different ways to solve every problem. If your ideal customer needs a job, you could teach him to start driving for Uber, coach him through a college degree, or write him the perfect résumé. But how do you choose the best category?

Here are a few ideas to get you started:

1. Talk with people

2. Find online communities

3. Try and fail

Let's look at each.

Talk with People

People love to talk. And when they do, a lot of complaints and questions pop up. You can use their words to spark ideas and clarify what problems they have. If you have some experience with the topic, you'll have good advice to share.

Spending time discussing the problem will often reveal a solution.

My favorite way to have customer conversations is called the "The 4HL Method" or the 4 Helpful Lists.

You ask 4 questions:

- What's right?

- What's wrong?

- What's confusing?

- What's missing?

By doing an interview with your ideal customer and asking them these questions about either your idea or existing products you can find a treasure chest full of useful information.

Let's do an example about shaving.

Here are some possible answers from customers.

1. What's right?

"I like when razors give a close shave without causing nicks or irritation."

"Having a razor that's easy to grip and maneuver around my face is great."

"I appreciate razors that stay sharp through multiple uses."

2. What's wrong?

"Buying razors in-store is too expensive, especially for good quality."

"I often forget to buy new blades until it's too late and I'm stuck with a dull shave."

"The big brands seem to charge a lot just for their name, not necessarily for a better product."

3. What's confusing?

"There are so many types and brands of razors, it's overwhelming to choose."

"I don't understand why some blades are so much more expensive than others."

"The difference between a 5-blade razor and a 3-blade isn't clear to me."

4. What's missing?

"A convenient, hassle-free way to get new razors without having to remember to shop for them."

"An affordable subscription service that delivers high-quality razors directly to my door."

"More transparency about what makes a good razor and why some are priced the way they are."

The end result? (of this pretend scenario)

Someone decided to create a Shave Club.

Find Online Communities

Talking to people one-on-one is great but time-consuming. You can also stalk—I mean *explore!*—online communities discussing your customer's problem. Seeing discussions in bulk helps you spot patterns faster than in individual conversations. Where these conversations take place doesn't matter—as long as members discuss your problem and your ideal customer hangs out there.

Don't stop with the obvious social media platforms. Explore niche-specific communities, too. Here is a quick list of places to get you started. As you go down this rabbit trail, also check out the resources that community members recommend.

- Facebook

- LinkedIn

- YouTube

- Reddit

- Quora

- Medium

- Substack

- Mighty Networks

Find the active communities, add value, interact, and spot the patterns while you search for solutions.

Try and Fail

How I wish I could save you the horror of trying and failing. But when building a business, you'll have to suffer through it.

You've got to try your solutions and fail until one works. Providing answers, helping for free, and checking results is the only way to validate your hypotheses.

Too often, we want to get paid for unproven concepts. But without evidence, you can't inspire confidence in your solutions, and you can't be sure you aren't making stuff up. Free trial runs help you prove that your solution works and give you excellent testimonials for marketing.

If it doesn't work, try a different solution. It took me one and a half years to nail my company's solution, but it was worth the wait. I know the customer, the problem, and my solution backward and forward.

You can, too.

ACTION STEP

It is time to select your niche.

This isn't a permanent decision. You'll likely pivot as you get wiser. But this niche will be your starting point in building a SIMPLE Online Business.

Review the chapter and implement what you've learned.

1. Choose Your Customer

Take a scrap of paper and jot down the answers to these questions. Whatever comes to mind will do.

- Who are you?

- Who were you?

- Who do you love?

Choose one of the persons you wrote down and fill in the blank below.

I'm going to serve (CUSTOMER).

EXAMPLE: I'm going to serve <u>busy dads</u>.

EXAMPLE: I'm going to serve <u>new independent insurance adjusters</u>.

2. Find a Problem You Want to Help Solve

Take another look at the three growth catalysts and brainstorm for customer problems.

- Bigger is better

- Smaller is faster

- First in series means bonus

Write down your ideal customer from action step 1, and scribble any customer problem you can think of. Once you have a winner, fill in the blanks below.

I want to help (INSERT CUSTOMER) with (PROBLEM)

EXAMPLE: I want to help <u>busy dads</u> with <u>knowing how to start an online business</u>.

EXAMPLE: I want to help <u>new independent insurance adjusters</u> with <u>getting work</u>.

If you can't find any problem you want to help your customer solve, have conversations until you do.

3. Keep an Open Mind for New Solutions & Choose a Category

Keeping an open mind is more of an attitude than an actionable step. You'll likely only discover a solution as you move on and dive deep into your niche.

You need to choose what direction or category of solutions you'll be pointing your customers to.

I will help (CUSTOMER)

solve (PROBLEM)

with (SOLUTION/CATEGORY)

EXAMPLE: I will help busy dads solve knowing how to start an online business with easy to follow frameworks.

EXAMPLE: I will help new independent insurance adjusters solve getting work with certifications and mentorship.

I hope you enjoyed this sample of the Simple Online Business Model. Head to the next page if you'd like to grab the full copy of the Simple Online Busines Model so you'll know exactly how to build an online business in your spare time.

Build Your
Business

Head to SimpleOnlineBusiness.com/book/ & learn how to build an online business using your book.

What You Should Read Next

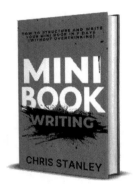

Mini Book Writing: How to Structure and Write Your Mini Book in 7 Days (Without Overthinking)

You can head to MiniBookStraitjacket.com to purchase the book.

Now that you are beginning to write your first mini book, I'd recommend reading Simple Online Business Model which you can find on Amazon. It guides you through how to build a niche online business that will grow using your mini book.

 If you've already read that and you are building your business and feeling the time pinch of balancing work and family, I recommend reading the Misleading Money Mantra. This book will help you learn how to build a business without sacrificing your life or family.

Books by Chris Stanley

Mini Book Publishing Series

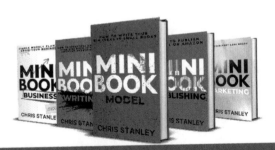

Mini Book Model: How to Write Your Big Ideas in Small Books[1]

---

1. https://minibookpublishing.com/

Mini Book Writing: How to Structure and Write Your Mini Book in 7 Days (Without Overthinking)[2]

Mini Book Publishing: How to Publish & Sell on Amazon[3]

Mini Book Marketing: Sell Your First 1,000 Books[4]

Mini Book Money: How to Turn 10,000 Words Into $10,000+

Simple Online Business Model: The Proven Roadmap to Finding Your Niche and Building a Profitable Online Business in Your Spare Time

Life Currencies Series

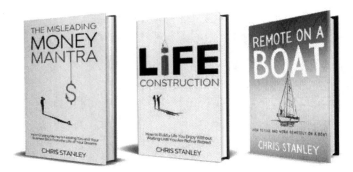

Misleading Money Mantra: How Chasing Money Is Holding You Back From the Life and Business of Your Dreams

Life Construction: How to Build a Life You Enjoy Without Waiting Until You Are Rich or Retired

Remote on a Boat: How to Live and Work remotely on a Boat (Coming Soon)

God is Like Devotional Series

God is Like a Geyser: 30 Day Devotional For When You Are Waiting on God or Geysers

God is Like a Rocket Launch: 30 Day Devotional For When You Are Looking for Purpose

God is Like a Democrat & a Republican: 30 Day Devotional for When You Need Reconciliation Due to Politics

God is Like a Virus: 30 Day Devotional About God's Viral Nature Through Human Interaction

God is Like 2020: 30 Day Devotional for People Who are Looking for God in the Chaos of the Year

God is Like a Video Game: 30 Day Devotional for Those Looking to Level Up Their Character

God is Like a Box of Crayons: 30-Day Devotional for When You Need a Brighter Day

God is Like a Box of Crayons Coloring Book: 30 Day Adult Coloring Book Devotional for When You Need a Brighter Day

God is Like Mining: 10 Day Unofficial Minecraft Devotional

Noob Angel Series (Unofficial Minecraft Bible Stories)

Noob Angel 01 David vs the Giant: Unofficial Minecraft & Bible Story

Noob Angel 02 Joshua and the Big Wall: Unofficial Minecraft & Bible Story

Sailing Adventures of Sol & Vox (SASV)

Doctopus the Pirate Octopus (Sailing Adventures of Sol & Vox Book 1)

Mermaid Palace of West Palm Beach (Sailing Adventures of Sol & Vox Book 2)

Vampires of Vero Beach (Sailing Adventures of Sol & Vox Book 3)

Insurance Adjuster (IA) Playbook Series

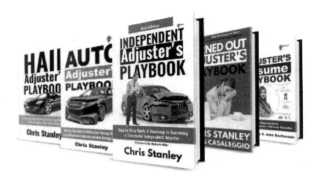

Independent Adjuster's Playbook: Step by Step Guide & Roadmap to Becoming a Successful Independent Adjuster

Auto Adjuster's Playbook: Step by Step Field Guide to Writing Auto Damage Estimates as an Independent Adjuster or Auto Damage Appraiser

Networking Adjuster's Playbook: Step by Step Guide & Journal to Successful Networking as an Independent Adjuster

Audatex Adjuster's Playbook: Step by Step Guide & Manual to Writing Auto Damage Estimates With Audatex

Hail Adjuster's Playbook: A Step by Step Guide to Being and Becoming a Catastrophic Independent Auto Hail Adjuster

Adjuster's Resume Playbook: A Step-by-Step Guide to Creating an Insurance Adjuster Resume

Insurance Company Adjuster's Playbook: A Career Guide for Getting Hired and Promoted as an Adjuster for an Insurance Company

Burned Out Adjuster's Playbook: Learn How to Stop Stressing and Start Enjoying Your Job As an Insurance Adjuster

PDR Cash Box: Insurance Adjuster Secrets For PDR Technicians: How to Increase Your Earnings and Lower Your Stress When Dealing with Insurance Companies & Shops

Made in the USA
Middletown, DE
29 July 2025

11380514R00071